4/17/96

Grades 4-6

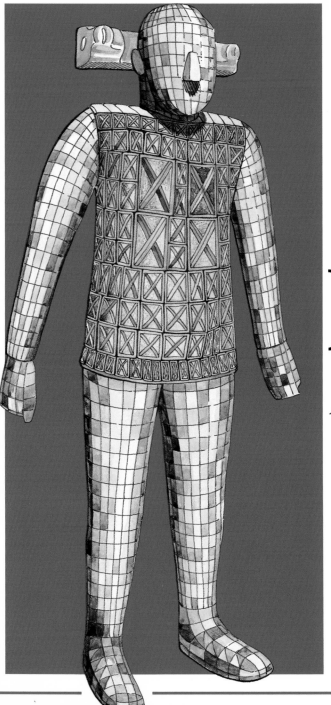

MUMMIES

A very peculiar history

SERIES EDITOR	DAVID SALARIYA
EDITOR	PENNY CLARKE
ASSISTANT	APRIL MCCROSKIE
ARTISTS	DAVID ANTRAM
	RAY BURROWS
	CHRIS ETHERIDGE
	GORDON MUNRO
	LEE PETERS
	CAROLYN SCRACE
	GERALD WOOD

DAVID SALARIYA has created many new series of books for publishers in the UK and overseas. In 1989 he established the Salariya Book Company.

NATHANIEL HARRIS has published a great many books and articles on historical and artistic subjects.

First published in the United States in 1995 by Franklin Watts

Franklin Watts
95 Madison Avenue
New York, NY 10016

© The Salariya Book Co. Ltd. MCMXCV

Library of Congress Cataloging-in-Publication Data

Harris, Nathaniel.
    Mummies : written by Nathaniel Harris : created and designed by David Salariya.
        p. cm. – (A very peculiar history)
    Summary: Overview of mummification and embalming including ancient beliefs regarding life after death, rites, rituals, and ceremonies, and the latest in the science of cryogenics.
    Includes index.
    ISBN 0-531-14354-6 (lib. bdg.)–
    ISBN 0-531-15271-5 (pbk.)
    1. Mummies–Juvenile literature.
2. Embalming–Juvenile literature.
[1. Mummies.] I. Salariya, David. II. Title.
III. Series
GN293.H37 1995
393'.3–dc20   94-39934
                                                    CIP
                                                    AC

Printed in Belgium

MUMMIES

A very peculiar history

Written by
NATHANIEL HARRIS

Created and designed by
DAVID SALARIYA

FRANKLIN WATTS

NEW YORK · CHICAGO · LONDON · TORONTO · SYDNEY

CONTENTS

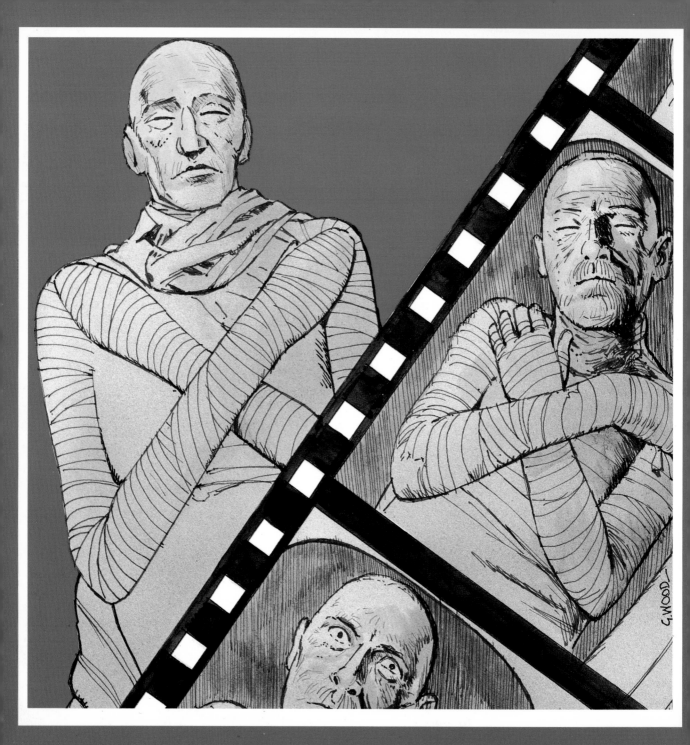

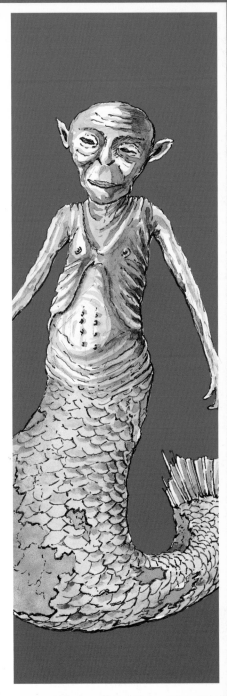

INTRODUCTION

A MUMMY IS A CORPSE that has been preserved from decay. This may be the result of human skill or, as you will see in the course of this book, may be completely unplanned and no more than a fortunate accident.

For most people, "mummy" conjures up images of ancient Egyptians, stretched out at full length and swathed in bandages. But the Egyptians were far from unique: mummies have existed in many places and periods. In these pages the reader will encounter English sailors and unknown Danes, Inuit and Incas, Scythians and Sicilians, a Chinese court lady, and an Alpine traveler. Some were expensively embalmed with chemicals; others were smoked, tanned, or frozen.

During their long afterlives, some of these preserved bodies, and parts of bodies, have suffered various mishaps. Oliver Cromwell lost his head soon *after* his death, and Lord Nelson was killed in battle and only then became sodden with drink! Jeremy Bentham, however, was more dignified, arranging that his skeleton should continue to attend college board meetings.

In the twentieth century embalmed leaders like Lenin have become objects of worship. Others, like Eva Perón, have been as politically powerful in death as in life. Now, the development of cryogenics (deep-freezing) has persuaded quite a few people to believe that they, like the Egyptians, can be preserved and, even, in time, live again. The peculiar history of mummies is clearly far from complete!

THE PROMISE OF ETERNITY

Every Egyptian hoped to live again after death — and in the flesh.

Ancient Egypt was "the gift of the Nile," which created a long fertile valley surrounded by desert.

ginger hair   sand pit

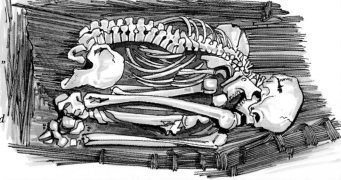

THE EGYPTIANS ENJOYED LIFE just as much as any other people in history. They were also intensely concerned with death and the afterlife and that was because they hoped to prolong their enjoyment into eternity. One of their main beliefs was that the human spirit could not survive death without a body which it would continue to inhabit on earth. As a result, great efforts were made to preserve a corpse, and the tomb became, for the dead person, very much like a house with every possible comfort.

Grand, multichambered tombs for the rich were built even before 3100 B.C., when Egypt was united under the first of its 30 royal dynasties. But in fact the bodies of these wealthy people, in their coffins and chambers, rotted in the normal way, while those of the poor, buried in the sand, dried out and survived. Eventually, the Egyptians realized just how effective dehydration could be as a preservative, and by about 2000 B.C. the first "man-made" Egyptian mummies had been created. Over the following centuries, embalming became a craft and ritual of great importance to Egyptian civilization.

THIS MAN (left) died 5,200 years ago, and was buried in the sand.

A BODY, buried at around the same date in a brick tomb (below), rapidly decayed in the usual way.

flint knife

Irreverently nicknamed "Ginger," this corpse (left) survived because it was buried in hot, dry sand. The sand absorbed all its fluids, leaving it bacteria-free.

THE EGYPTIANS BELIEVED that the first mummy was the murdered god Osiris (left), who was bandaged up by his sister Isis. He became king of the underworld and judge of the dead.

(Right) A symbol of rebirth: the boy pharaoh Tutankhamen emerges from the head of a lotus.

painted plaster

EGYPTIAN EMBALMERS had their triumphs and also their setbacks. The mummy of the great warrior pharaoh Amosis I (right) shows how effectively they could preserve a body by the sixteenth century B.C. Although looking somewhat older than he did at the time of his death, Amosis is still in better condition than Queen Henttawy (below), who was embalmed by a more elaborate technique 500 years later. The skin of her face was packed to restore its fullness, but the embalmers overdid this, with the result that the stuffing burst through the skin.

arthritic knees

"mummy" style

artificial black hair

traces of rouge

stuffing

bandages

THE EMBALMER'S ART

Embalming was done in booths set up on the west bank of the Nile river.

On its arrival at the embalmer's booth on the west bank of the Nile, the corpse was ritually purified with water.

While the corpse was being prepared, the "ripper" waited to open up the body and remove the internal organs.

Having finished, the ripper was driven away with curses. Though useful, his bloody work insulted the gods.

Next, the body was washed. Covering and packing it with natron crystals took time and care.

FOR CENTURIES, mummification was a privilege enjoyed only by the pharaoh and a few favorites. But from about 2500 B.C. many more people were able to hope for immortality by having themselves embalmed, although mummification remained an expensive business, well beyond the means of most Egyptians.

Embalming was a religious rite as well as a practical operation. It was presided over by a priest who wore a jackal mask representing Anubis, the god of embalming, and every significant stage in the proceedings was accompanied by the chanting of prayers and spells.

A first-class embalming took seventy days. The first forty were devoted to extracting every drop of moisture from the body to leave no breeding ground for the bacteria that caused decay. The soft internal organs and the brain were removed, then the body was packed and covered with natron, a form of natural salt, and left on the embalming table to dry out. After forty days it was blackened and shriveled, but potentially immortal.

THE JACKAL-HEADED Anubis (right) was the Egyptian god of embalming, intimately involved in the rituals surrounding funerals and burials. The chief embalmer would have worn a pottery mask like this. It has two eyeholes beneath the jaws.

hollow mask

Resembling sinister knitting needles, these implements (below) were used to draw the brains out of the corpse's skull.

A flint knife (above) was used to make a cut in the body of the dead person so that the internal organs could be removed.

tool in nostril

stitching

The brain was removed by pulling it down through the nostril (left).

brain hook

A LONG INCISION was made in the left side of the corpse, and the lungs, stomach, liver, and intestines were removed through it. When the body was ready for bandaging, the edges of the incision were drawn together and covered with a foil or wax plate carrying a protective symbol, the wadjet. Unusually, the wound here has been sewn up.

passage to brain

falcon   jackal   baboon

The internal organs were stored in four canopic jars (left). Each was guarded by a "Son of Horus" in the form of a baboon (lungs), jackal (stomach), human (liver), and falcon (intestines).

Bags of natron (below), ready for use. Natron was a natural salt, mainly consisting of sodium carbonate and sodium bicarbonate. All the materials used in embalming were carefully collected and buried near the corpse.

human

An embalming table (left, below) on which a corpse dried out.

lion head

basin to collect fluids

Bound for the Tomb

A mummy went into eternity wrapped in as much as 3,850 sq ft (375 sq m) of bandaging.

The body was packed, plumped out, and covered with molten resin. Often the entire body was painted, with red ocher for a man, yellow for a woman.

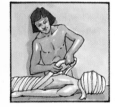

Bandaging followed a prescribed ritual, beginning with the head, and took at least fifteen days. Each layer was waterproofed with a coating of resin.

Finally a red burying cloth or shroud was wrapped tightly around the mummy. Then a painted portrait mask was placed over its head.

EVERY EGYPTIAN had several spirits, or souls. After death they could find their way back to the right body only if they could tell it apart from other mummies. So when the corpse had been dried out, it underwent a restorative beauty treatment. The skin was massaged to make it supple again, the body was stuffed and perfumed, and padding was inserted under the skin as a substitute for plump, living flesh. Finally the face was made up.

All this was done for the sole benefit of spirit eyes, for the next stage was to coat the mummy in protective resin and then wrap it from head to foot in layer after layer of bandages and shrouds. To make sure that the spirits would have no difficulty in identifying their destined home, a portrait mask was placed over the head and shoulders of the mummy. Thus dressed up, it was ready for its long journey into the afterlife.

In its final stages, the embalmers' work involved the use of layers of wrappings and the individual bandaging of limbs and other body parts. Prayers and spells were chanted at the most solemn moments.

bags of natron

EACH TOE of the boy pharaoh Tutankhamen (right) was inserted into a gold sheath, marked with grooves to suggest nails and skin creases. Sandals of beaten gold were placed on his feet, which were then wrapped in linen.

all-gold thong

toe sheath

(Far left) Late in ancient Egyptian history, around 300 B.C., superbly lifelike encaustic (wax paint) portraits of the dead person were placed over the mummy's head or on the coffin.

But by this time a showy exterior had come to be regarded as all-important, and the actual embalming was often shoddily done.

X rays showed that one lady (left) had been interred with someone else's skull between her legs!

spare skull

Amulets were bandaged in with the mummy, to protect it in the afterlife.

(Right) Parts that became detached during the embalming might be reattached, like these teeth, carefully held together by gold wire.

gold wire

(Above) Luxury substitutes: eyes and a tongue of gold leaf might be placed in the sockets and mouth of a noble client.

When more people wished to be embalmed, name tags (above) were attached to identify each mummy.

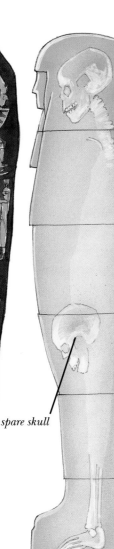

THE INDIVIDUALLY WRAPPED toes of the warrior pharaoh Ramses II, who died c.1223 B.C. A brilliant general and ruthless ruler, Ramses II extended the empire of ancient Egypt.

wrapped in finest linen

INTO THE AFTERLIFE

The essentials: mummification, proper burial, and a safe journey through the underworld.

(Above) An adze was a tool used in the Opening of the Mouth ceremony.

(Above) A dead man, Sennedjen, stands at the gate to the other world.

BEARERS CARRY food and goods to the tomb, while hired mourners wail and tear at their hair.

The Opening of the Mouth ceremony took place at the entrance to the tomb. The touching of the "lips" with symbolic implements enabled the dead to see and feel again.

WHEN THE seventy-day embalming was over, the mummy was put in a coffin, which was placed within a shrine and carried in procession to the tomb. A priest led the way, accompanied by grieving relatives and loudly wailing professional mourners. Behind, bearers brought food offerings and a variety of possessions for the dead person's use in the afterlife. At the tomb entrance, the coffin was held upright and the priest performed the vital Opening of the Mouth ceremony to restore the body's senses and allow its departed soul to return. Then, with much ceremony, the coffin was placed in the tomb.

However, a happy afterlife was only certain once the soul had made a perilous journey through the underworld, identifying various gods and chanting the appropriate spells; these were written on the coffin, or on papyrus rolls (the "Book of the Dead") in the tomb. Finally, the soul faced judgment: the dead person's heart was weighed, with Ammut the devourer waiting to pounce. If it passed the test, one of its spirits, the *akh*, joined the immortals, while other, personal and important spirits, the *ka* and the *ba*, lived on in the tomb.

In life, a pharaoh was believed to be an incarnation of the gods Horus and Osiris. So Osiris's mother, Nut, greets Tutankhamen in the afterlife as her son.

Upraised arms symbolized the ka, *a sort of spirit double of the dead person.*

WEIGHING the heart. Having threaded a way through the underworld, the dead person was led to the scales by Anubis, who weighed the heart against the feather of truth. The result was recorded by the ibis-headed god Thoth.

The ba *rejoining the mummy in the tomb. The* ba, *pictured as a human-headed bird, was the most "personal" of a person's several souls or spirits.*

— Anubis

Thoth

Ammut

heart

feather

scarab beetle symbolizing rebirth

Reaping the reward of righteousness (left). Sennedjen, who stood in fear at the gate to the other world (opposite page) is reunited with his wife Iynefert in the Fields of the Blessed.

The heart scarab (above) was probably the most vital of the mummy's amulets. At the weighing of the heart, its power prevented the heart from giving away the dead person's secrets.

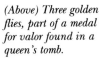

AT HOME WITH THE DEAD

With care and foresight, an Egyptian's afterlife became a pleasant prospect.

(Above) Three golden flies, part of a medal for valor found in a queen's tomb.

(Right) Leisure and luxury persisted into eternity: Queen Kawit is shown at breakfast while maids serve her and arrange her wig.

(Right) Party time in the afterlife. Dancers perform nearly naked, a flautist plays, girls clap, and a lavish spread is provided.

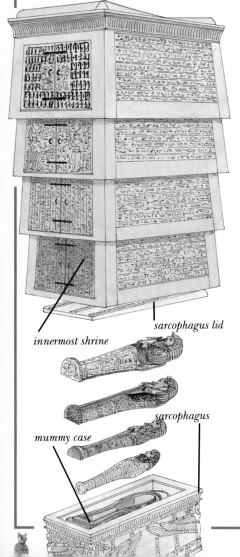

innermost shrine

sarcophagus lid

mummy case

sarcophagus

THE TOMB was an Egyptian's "eternal home," but it was not a prison. One spirit of the dead person, the *ka*, remained permanently in residence, but the *ba* was free to roam at will during the day, returning each night to the mummified body. And even within the tomb there were pleasures and pastimes, magically available in the form of paintings and models, which enabled the dead to join in a feast or cruise down the Nile, relaxing in a cabin while model sailors did the work.

Nor was contact lost with the outside world. It was the duty of the relatives of the dead to set out food and drink for the *ka*, and to make visits and offerings on feast days. However, the Egyptians were well aware that everyone is forgotten in time, so they filled the tomb with objects that served as a form of insurance against this. Painted and modeled food provided a substitute for absent offerings, and if the mummy itself decayed, the statue of the deceased and the human-form mask and coffins would help the wandering *ba* to recognize its home.

(Left) Everything was done to enable a pharaoh to rest in splendor and security. His masked mummy lay in a nest of coffins, encased in a stone sarcophagus which in turn stood within great shrines-within-shrines.

This mummy mask (right) probably belonged to an Egyptian princess. The pharaoh's mummy was covered with a gold mask, but this is made of a kind of papier-mâché called cartonnage, finely molded and gilded.

— wig

— underworld scenes

Queen Nefertari (right) plays sennet, a board game which also symbolized the soul's attempt to win through to the afterlife. (Below) One of three sets buried with Tutankhamen.

— sennet piece

wood and ivory board

image of Tutankhamen

A pharaoh's earrings (above), designed for pierced lobes. Made of gold and other materials, these were found in the tomb of Tutankhamen.

(Left) In solitary grandeur, a stone sarcophagus stands in its bare cave tomb. Intrepid robbers soon deprived the pharaohs of their treasures.

Shabti figures (left) were put into the tomb to do any work the gods might demand.

woven string

This outer coffin (above) held the mummy of a Libyan who settled in Egypt. The central strip carries scenes in which the dead man makes his way through the underworld into the presence of Osiris.

This folding bed with copper hinges and animal legs was found in Tutankhamen's tomb.

FAMOUS EGYPTIAN MUMMIES

After three millennia, these gaunt figures still have a powerful individuality.

From c.1500 B.C. pharaohs were buried in the Valley of the Kings.

This elderly woman (below), still full of character, may be Queen Tiye, mother of the pharaoh Akhenaton.

ALTHOUGH MANY EGYPTIANS enjoyed the afterlife for thousands of years, robbers and vandals eventually destroyed most of them. The best preserved surviving mummies are pharaohs and their relatives, more carefully embalmed and more zealously looked after than lesser immortals. Even these date mainly from late in ancient Egyptian history, 1550-1070 B.C., when pyramid tombs were abandoned for less accessible resting places, cut deep into the cliffs of the Valley of the Kings near the Nile river. When these failed to foil tomb robbers, priests decided to safeguard the mummies – though not their treasures – by moving them in groups to other tombs, where they lay until they were discovered in the nineteenth century. Among them were warrior pharaohs such as Seti I and Ramses II. Ironically, the best known to us today is a minor ruler who died young, Tutankhamen. His tomb, almost intact, was opened in 1922.

Yuya (above) and his wife Thuya are among the best-preserved of all mummies. As the parents of Queen Tiye, they were buried in the Valley of the Kings.

(Right) The gold death mask of the boy pharaoh Tutankhamen, one of the fabulous treasures found in 1922.

TUTANKHAMEN's mummy (right) is in poor condition, in contrast to the golden splendor of his tomb.

THE BANDAGES on the hands and arms of Ramses II (below) are splendidly preserved. His sticklike limbs give a misleading impression, since he lived to be almost ninety and fathered scores of children.

padded cheeks

separately bandaged fingers

resin-darkened skin

In the tenth century B.C. the embalmers gave Queen Nodjmet (above) the cosmetic treatment. However, they padded out her cheeks so much that she looks grotesque rather than lifelike.

(Right) Seti I, still self-possessed and majestic in death. One of the greatest pharaohs, Seti carried Egyptian power as far as Syria and defeated the Libyans. He fathered another warrior pharaoh, Ramses II. Seti's tomb is shown on page 36.

well preserved features

PICTURED as a larger-than-life hero, Ramses II holds prisoners by their hair.

EVEN A PHARAOH who never fought in battle was shown as a victor in his chariot.

S. WOOD

19

THE MUMMY'S CURSE

Treasures, tombs, and mummies: the ancient Egyptian formula for a modern myth.

(Above) Tomb robbing is a trade as old as the tombs themselves. A peasant woman looks for treasures, apparently indifferent to her grisly surroundings.

(Left) "Take one foot, grind down and mix in while stirring all the while…": mummy was much used by medieval alchemists for cure-alls such as the elixir of life.

IF THEY COULD SPEAK, Egypt's mummies might declare that they – not those who violated their tombs – were the victims of a curse. In antiquity, robbers tore mummies open to take their jewels. During the Middle Ages, thanks to their supposedly magical properties, mummies were ground down or boiled up for powders and potions. Later still, European treasure hunters blundered about in their tombs, crunching brittle bodies underfoot. Mummies were unwrapped and casually discarded as after-dinner entertainment for tourists. And even industry did its worst, using mummies' bandages to make paper and their resin-steeped bodies for fuel. Yet there were also some people who responded with a thrill to the Egyptians' quest for eternity. In the nineteenth century, stories of mummies coming back to life, with fateful consequences, were published by authors such as Edgar Allan Poe and Conan Doyle. The groundwork for a modern myth was well laid by 1922, when the tomb of Tutankhamen was opened and the seal of the pharaoh's shrine was broken by British archaeologist Howard Carter. Soon afterward, the death of his backer, Lord Carnarvon, gave rise to the legend of a fatal curse, kept alive ever since by newspapers, novels, and the movies.

(Below) Unopened for three thousand years: handles on the doors of the third of Tutankhamen's shrines.

(LEFT) One of the few genuinely sinister objects to survive from ancient Egypt is the "screaming mummy." To judge from his expression, this man was asphyxiated and so must have been buried alive – probably as a punishment since he was wrapped in sheepskin which often denoted a criminal.

rope still knotted

(Right) European tourists visited Egypt from as early as the seventeenth century. Most treated everything they found with thoughtless brutality.

THE LEGEND of the mummy's curse grew after the death of Lord Carnarvon, who financed the archaeological digs which led to the discovery of Tutankhamen's tomb in November 1922. Carnarvon was present at the opening of the tomb. So, was his death four months later "King Tut's revenge"?

HOWARD CARTER, the British archaeologist who discovered Tutankhamen's tomb and opened its innermost shrine (left). Had the mummy's curse existed, he should have been its victim, but he survived for another 17 years, dying in 1939.

Carnarvon's real killer was the mosquito (above) that bit him on the cheek. Blood poisoning followed, and pneumonia killed him.

Ramses III

"The Mummy"

The "curse" was a blessing to movies. In "The Mummy," Boris Karloff, entombed like the "screaming mummy" opposite, returned from the dead in the twentieth century. His appearance was based on that of Ramses III's mummy.

(Above) The seal, still bearing its original stamp – but no curse.

YIELDING THEIR SECRETS

Interrogated through postmortems and X rays, mummies have much to tell.

Egyptians entered the afterlife with terrible teeth, often worn down to the nerves.

(Above) Coarsely ground corn, with wind-blown sand in it, ruined teeth.

Seti I, all-conquering pharaoh and the father of a warrior.

Ramses II, even in mummified form, is un-mistakably Seti's son.

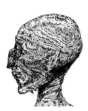

Merenptah, Seti's grandson: the family likeness persists.

(Right) The pharaoh Siptah barely survived into manhood, but his most obvious disability was his deformed left foot. Analysis suggests that it was the result of polio.

BY THE TIME scientific investigation of Egyptian mummies began, in the late nineteenth century, relatively few were still in good condition. From 1895, X rays made it possible to examine the interior of a mummy without damaging it. Now, thanks to new scientific methods, mummies can be probed by virtually nondestructive CAT scans (cross-sectional X rays), endoscope viewing via the throat, DNA sampling, and radiocarbon dating.

As a result, our knowledge of Egyptian family relationships has been established on better evidence than that of the hooked noses, buck teeth, or curved spines shared by members of some dynasties. The age and general appearance of a pharaoh, what he ate, and (sometimes) how he died may be inferred. Knowledge of the Egyptians' ailments, their bad teeth, and arthritic complaints, helps to build a picture of ancient society and should dispel any illusions we may have about the Good Old Days!

Ramses V died in his thirties. The scars caused by smallpox are still visible.

deformed left foot

(Right) Seqenenre Tao's horrific wounds were inflicted by axes, clubs, and maces, suggesting he died in battle. Forensic analysis showed that he had survived an earlier head wound, which had probably left him partly paralyzed.

cheek wound

NATSUF-AMUN (below) was a priest and scribe at Karnak who died in his mid-forties. He was quite tall, had dental problems, and somehow lost his nose. His protruding tongue remains a mystery. Was he strangled or did a bite make his tongue swell?

priestly shaven head

skull wounds

missing nose

protruding tongue

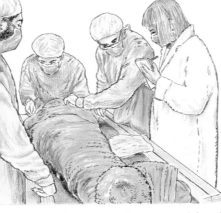

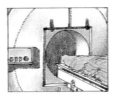

(Above) A mummy slides into the CAT scanner, a radiological machine developed in the 1960s. It provides cross-sectional views of the mummy's contents.

THE DISSECTION of a mummy (above) offers the most direct scientific evidence, but destroys the mummy. Normally it is done only if the mummy is badly decayed.

shaven chin

wrappings

(Left) This painstaking reconstruction of the original appearance of a mummified teenager was the work of a Manchester University team. It is based on evidence such as a bone defect likely to have made breathing through the nose difficult; hence the girl's open-mouthed, adenoidal look.

MADE TO LAST

Embalming, an age-old craft, has been practiced all over the world.

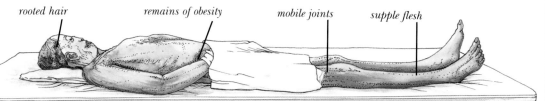

stitching

leaping animals

This elaborate tattoo on the right arm of an embalmed Scythian chief proclaims his status; from a Siberian tomb.

rooted hair   *remains of obesity*   *mobile joints*   *supple flesh*

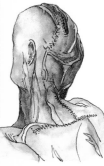

(Above) Embalming was a skilled operation even in remote Siberia. This woman's skin has been carefully sewn up following trepanning.

Smoked and given a protective coating of clay that is still regularly renewed, these mummified ancestors (right) sit on scaffolding, perched on a cliff above their home village in Papua New Guinea. The fluids extracted during their mummification are used as massage gel.

THERE ARE FORMS OF behavior that seem to appear at some stage in the history of almost every culture. Human sacrifice and waging war are among them, and so is mummification of the dead. In fact the practice is so widespread that it suggests the existence of a universal human impulse toward self-preservation beyond death. Egyptian embalming was done because the material body was thought to play a vital role in the afterlife. Different attitudes have not inhibited the embalming of medieval English royalty or, more recently, the mummification of professional people in Sicily. Techniques, however, vary. Papua New Guineans smoke-cured their ancestors like kippers while the Guanche Indians of the Canary Islands preserved their dead as meticulously as the ancient Egyptians. Finally, though mummification has generally reflected the reverence felt by the living for the dead, headhunters in some cultures have operated in a rather different spirit, preserving the shriveled remains of their victims as trophies.

Lady Dai lived in China two thousand years ago. Salted and buried in a nest of coffins packed with charcoal, she is superbly preserved.

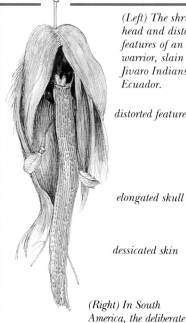

(Left) The shrunken head and distorted features of an enemy warrior, slain by the Jivaro Indians of Ecuador.

distorted features

(Left) Stone tombs on a mountainside in Peru. Their occupants were mummified and, as in ancient Egypt, were well provided with offerings of food.

upright stance

wig

elongated skull

dessicated skin

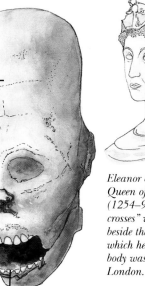

statue at Lincoln

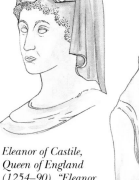

(Right) In South America, the deliberate mummification of the dead is a very old practice. This skull, elongated by binding at birth, comes from the ancient Nazca culture of south Peru c.200 B.C. to A.D. 500.

worn-down teeth

Eleanor of Castile, Queen of England (1254–90). "Eleanor crosses" were erected beside the route along which her embalmed body was taken to London.

(Right) This mummy is one of several thousands inhabiting the catacombs of the Convent of the Capuchins in Palermo, Sicily. Embalming by the monks began in the sixteenth century and went on until 1881.

(Left) In the catacombs of Palermo the dead lie on shelves or stand in line. Booking a place in the catacombs was fashionable among the middle class.

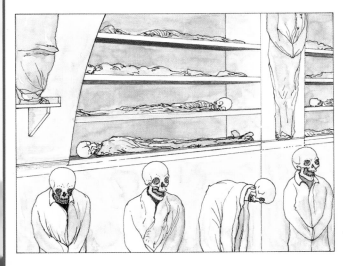

IN THE TIME CAPSULE

Victims and heroes, separated by five millennia but frozen in time.

The Iceman's flint dagger and its woven grass sheath.

This Inca boy was a human sacrifice. He may have been drugged before being abandoned high in the Andes.

deerskin

quiver

arrows

Mistaken for a modern casualty, the Iceman endured some rough handling when he was hauled from his frozen tomb. Later, archaeologists thought that he came from the Bronze Age (c.2200 B.C.), until the blade of his axe made them realize that he was even older. He was tattooed, dark-haired and about 5 feet (1.6m) tall; his fingernails were carefully clipped. His clothes were insulated with straw and his knapsack held provisions and a first-aid kit.

NOT ALL MUMMIES have been deliberately embalmed. Some have been preserved by accident, or at any rate without human intervention. Early Egyptians such as "Ginger" (page 8) dried out in hot sand, but elsewhere mummification was often the result of freezing, through being encased in ice or through the action of intensely cold, dry winds. Whereas embalming normally involves the destruction of the "soft" organs, freezing preserves an unnervingly human appearance. This is true of "the Iceman," an Alpine traveler who probably died of exhaustion – perhaps overtaken by bad weather – around 3000 B.C., and was discovered in 1991. His well-filled kit bag makes him seem like a modern backpacker. In the Andes, the natural positions and sleepy expressions of children left as sacrifices to mountain gods, make them seem hauntingly alive. By contrast, there is horror in the curled lips and bared teeth of nineteenth-century British mariners exhumed from their Arctic graves.

DRUGGED or strangled, this youth was buried as a sacrifice to Andean spirits. Only the top of his head poked out from the rocks – which was why he was discovered, and also why the flesh over his skull had decayed.

JOHN TORRINGTON (right) was one of three men buried on Beechey Island in the Canadian Arctic, where Sir John Franklin's expedition wintered in 1845-46. Their frozen bodies were exhumed in 1984.

blue striped shirt

THE INCAS honored their sacrificial victims, burying them with rich offerings such as this silver llama and a statuette of a goddess.

typical crouched position

The first sight of Able Seaman John Hartnell (right), still encased in ice after 138 years. Like Torrington, he lies on Beechey Island.

linen trousers

emaciated features

big toes tied together

preserved eyeballs

Close-up of Torrington's head. One of the first expeditions to have canned food; defects in the canning process may have given them lead poisoning.

THE GREENLAND MUMMIES

Eight bodies lay in sheltered Arctic graves, preserved by cold and wind.

(Above) Greenland. The mummies were discovered at Qilakitsoq, on the west coast.

THE FROZEN Greenlanders lay in two graves which were close together. The bodies lay stacked on top of one another. In the grave with five bodies, the small child lay on top, immediately above the four-year-old boy, who seems to have suffered from Down Syndrome.

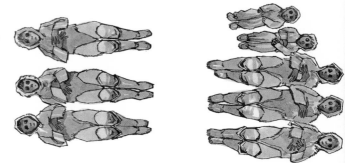

sealskin parka

preserved skin and brows

THE INUIT, OR ESKIMOS, successfully colonized the lands beyond the Arctic Circle. They adapted to the cold, hostile climate, developing a hunting culture that for centuries produced better results than European efforts to cultivate the soil in these regions. In Greenland, which the Inuit reached from the west by about A.D. 1000, they eventually displaced the struggling European settlements altogether. Evidence of the Inuit past has survived, but the first really well-preserved mummies were discovered only in 1972, at the abandoned settlement of Qilakitsoq on the west coast of Greenland.

Two Greenlanders out hunting found a grave with the bodies of five people in it, and another was uncovered close by with three people in it. The graves were sheltered by an overhanging rock, and low temperatures and dry, dehydrating winds had kept the bodies in excellent condition. The "Greenland Mummies" consisted of a child six months old, a boy of four, and six women of various ages. A thorough scientific investigation dated the bodies to about 1475.

(Left) Still an endearing figure, the six-month-old boy is the best preserved of the Greenland Mummies: being so small, he would have lost body heat much faster than the adults. It is possible that his mother died, and that he was put into the grave, alive, with her.

kamiks

(Left) The teeth of the older women were ravaged by years of use as tools to part sinews and scrape or soften sealskin.

slab of sealskin

(Right) The women's sealskin inner trousers.

This sealskin parka, one of 24 found in the graves, shows that the design of Inuit clothing has not changed much over a period of several hundred years.

hood

front seam

gathered and stitched sole

Tattooing on all but one of the women's faces showed up under infrared photography. One of the younger women looked something like this.

(Above) The Greenland Mummies's boots (kamiks) were skin legs onto which soles were sewn.

(Right) The head louse is a parasite. It was mummified along with its host.

THIS WOMAN of about thirty (below) is well wrapped up for her journey to the Land of the Dead. The Inuit spirit had to be purified before being admitted on the "other side." So the eight Greenlanders were buried with 78 items of clothing, ready for a long and difficult journey.

dark sealskin sleeve

skin cut to form "tail"

sealskin trousers

well-kept hands

detachable hood

THE BOG PEOPLE

The faces of Iron Age men and women, revealed after two thousand years.

Grauballe Man's hand and foot were beautifully preserved.

(Below) Tollund Man was also found in Denmark. Despite his jaunty cap and apparently serene expression, he was a sacrificial victim, hanged before being cast into the bog with the halter still around his neck. Such victims went virtually naked to their deaths. Tollund Man's possessions were only his cap and belt, and the noose that hanged him.

WHEN A BODY is uncovered in the depths of a bog, the finders call in the police. They are usually right to suspect foul play; but the dark deed may well prove to be two thousand years old, so the case is handed over to archaeologists. A corpse can survive indefinitely in a peat bog because the spongy layers keep out the oxygen which causes organic matter to decompose. Instead, soil acids tan the body, giving it a distinctively tough, brown, leathery but still disturbingly lifelike appearance.

Peat cutters in northwest Europe have uncovered hundreds of these "bog people," but only in recent years have archaeologists managed to photograph and perhaps preserve the remains. The most sensational finds have been of Iron Age people – Celtic or Germanic contemporaries of the Romans who lived between about 400 B.C. and A.D. 400. Most of them died by violence, as ritual sacrifices.

(Above) Grauballe Man, an Iron Age Dane, had his throat cut almost from ear to ear. His form is distorted because soil acids ate away the bones of bog people, so that in time the peat covering squashed and stretched their bodies without destroying them. By contrast, Grauballe Man's fingerprints are as distinct as any living man's.

Lindow Man when he was found (far left) and as forensic evidence suggests that he looked in life. The best-preserved British bog person, he was discovered in 1984 at Lindow in Cheshire. Nicknamed "Pete Marsh," his sacrifice was violent: he was struck three times on the head, his jugular was severed and, while the blood spurted out, he was garroted (strangled).

(Right) Horn comb found with a bog victim.

zigzag decoration

(Left) The delicate net cap worn by a young victim over her abundant, piled-up hair.

half-shaven head

ox-hide collar

(Above, right) Torcs (neck ornaments) were often thrown into bogs as offerings, and their circular, twisted design may recall the nooses used on the bog people.

This girl of about 14 (right), from Windeby, north Germany, may have been a "criminal" rather than a sacrifice. Her head was half-shaved and she was blindfolded before being drowned weighted down with stones and branches.

woven blindfold

twisted string ties

A STRANGE WAY TO GO

Bodies for whom death was not – quite – the end.

England's naval hero, Horatio Nelson, was killed at the battle of Trafalgar, 1805.

Unheroic but efficient: Nelson's body was brought home in a cask of brandy.

Transferred to a lead coffin, his remains were buried at St. Paul's.

The brandy worked so well that it was possible to make Nelson's death mask.

ONCE GONE, MOST OF US ARE QUICKLY REMOVED FROM PUBLIC VIEW, with or without ceremony or regret. But sometimes the dead stay out in the world for a time and even play a part in its affairs. Corpses have been kept in the house by relatives who could not bear to part with them, put on display, or set up on thrones long after their deaths, to prove their claims. But only a few have known the glory of the eleventh-century Spanish warrior El Cid, said to have been so feared that, when he died, his corpse was strapped to his horse and sent into battle, causing the enemy host to flee in confusion.

Posthumous "lives" are not always so honorable. A good old English custom, abandoned only in the nineteenth century, was to leave the bodies of executed persons at crossroads, hanging in chains until they rotted, as a warning to passing travelers who might have criminal intentions. There is evidently a powerful symbolism involved in debasing a dead body, for in many cases a corpse has been specially dug up for the purpose and even, like Pope Formosus I, put on trial before "execution"!

King Charles I (1600–49), who really was executed, faced a different problem: what to do about his head. A deeply religious man, he feared that on the final Day of Judgment, when God chose people to go to heaven, he would not be chosen if he were headless. To overcome this problem he arranged for embalmers to reattach his head to his body after his beheading.

(Left) The Spanish hero El Cid's corpse was strapped to his horse, helping his troops to win a last victory.

The Scottish explorer David Livingstone (left) died in Africa in 1873. His followers buried his heart before taking his body back to the coast.

(Right) The seventeenth-century diarist Samuel Pepys recorded that on his thirty-sixth birthday "I did kiss a queen" – the embalmed body of Queen Katherine, dead since 1437.

(Right) The philosopher Jeremy Bentham (1748–1832) left his skeleton to University College, London, along with his mummified head. Fully dressed, and with a wax "face," it long attended college board meetings.

Gala Dalí's body was propped up and driven to her castle at Pubol so she could "die" and be buried there.

TALES OF BODILY PARTS

Sometimes the part survives the whole, and has its own adventures.

At Jericho, in about 6000 B.C., the skulls of the dead were covered with plaster modeled to mimic a face, with shell "eyes."

OUR ANCESTORS had contradictory attitudes toward the dead. Within Christianity, for example, there was a powerful tradition that the body was unworthy; yet the remains of holy people were felt to be so full of spiritual power that even a few bones or a tiny organ were venerated and eagerly sought after. So great was the demand, in fact, that saints rarely stayed all in one piece, but were distributed throughout Christendom. Each body part was enshrined in a splendid casket or reliquary.

The opposite of veneration was, of course, desecration – decapitation, the cutting off of hands, or castration. The head was most often preserved as a trophy or displayed in grinning triumph; and when it had deteriorated too far, it was always possible to drink from the skull. Since ancient Egyptian times, the heart has always had a special significance. The Scottish king Robert the Bruce (1274–1329) wanted his heart to make a pilgrimage to the Holy Land and, it is said, that at his cremation in 1822, the dead poet Shelley's heart would not burn. By contrast, the brain has never been much valued – an odd comment on human nature.

RELIQUARY, said to contain the finger that "Doubting Thomas" thrust into Jesus's side.

(Below) A reliquary, set with enamels and precious stones; it is said to hold the foot of St. Andrew.

Oliver Cromwell (1599–1658) was buried in one piece, but later his royalist enemies dug him up and put his head on display (left).

SIR JAMES DOUGLAS carried the heart of the Scottish king Robert the Bruce on its way to the Holy Land. However, caught up in a battle in Spain, he flung the casket containing the heart into the fray.

Doubly macabre, this book (above) recounts the dissection of the nineteenth-century murderer John Horwood – and is bound in his own skin. The stylized gibbet on the cover adds a final ghoulish touch.

(Left) "Waterloo teeth": in the nineteenth century the teeth of soldiers who fell in battle were commonly removed and used to make dentures.

FRANKENSTEIN'S "monster" (right). In Mary Shelley's nineteenth-century novel "he" was constructed from many different body parts.

SCOUNDRELS AND SCIENTISTS

Tombs and their treasures have always attracted the unscrupulous, often with fatal results.

(Above) Even in antiquity, tomb robbers were tireless in climbing every obstacle, avoiding traps and defying taboos.

(Below) Dissection of the human body had been forbidden for centuries. In the seventeenth century, when Rembrandt painted his "anatomy lessons," only the corpses of criminals could be used for dissection.

The tomb of Seti I (below and right) was cut into the rock of the Valley of the Kings. Although hundreds of feet long, and concealed beyond a deep pit and false passage, it was robbed like the other royal tombs.

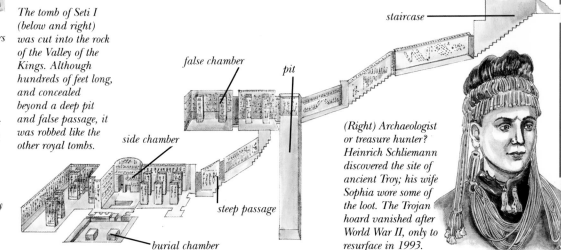

staircase

false chamber

pit

side chamber

steep passage

burial chamber

(Right) Archaeologist or treasure hunter? Heinrich Schliemann discovered the site of ancient Troy; his wife Sophia wore some of the loot. The Trojan hoard vanished after World War II, only to resurface in 1993.

FILLING TOMBS with treasures is a natural expression of respect for the dead, and of belief in an afterlife where possessions and status continue to matter. Unfortunately, a splendid burial does not necessarily mean that the body "rests in peace," as the ancient Egyptians discovered. Tomb robbing is an old profession. Never minding the terrors of a spirit-inhabited tomb, ingenious false leads, and the threat of death by impalement if they were caught, generations of Egyptian robbers did a thorough job, long before treasure hunters, tourists, and archaeologists came along.

The same fate befell tombs elsewhere. Generally speaking, the robbers were not interested in the dead, although the bodies might suffer accidental damage or be roughly handled if there were valuables on them. But in the eighteenth century the development of anatomy as a science led to a very gruesome development. Legally permitted to dissect only the corpses of executed murderers, anatomists began a no-questions-asked trade with bodysnatchers ... who did not always wait for their victims to die naturally.

(ABOVE) EXTRACTED from her "final" resting place by the bodysnatchers, this newly buried corpse will soon be on her way to an anatomist's dissecting table.

HER BONES still lavishly adorned with gold, this young woman was discovered in 1978 in Afghanistan, evidence of a wealthy and ancient society.

BODYSNATCHERS (right) developed their own professional skills. Since anatomists were only interested in fresh corpses, the "resurrection men" watched out for funerals, returning late at night to empty the grave. Instead of shifting all the earth above the coffin, they dug a shaft at its head, pried it open with iron hooks, and pulled the body up the shaft—an operation that only took about an hour.

(Below) Tomb robbers and treasure hunters are not always human. Magpies are notorious thieves of bright objects; but few have equaled the mice who packed their burrows with little, light, flat disks of pure gold, taken from the tombs in Afghanistan.

William Burke (right) and William Hare sold bodies to the Edinburgh anatomist Dr. Robert Knox.

skeleton of Hare

gold crown

gold tunic disks

WHERE'S THAT BODY?

Some no-bodies, including fakes, stand-ins, plaster casts, and "hollow men."

Hominid footprints from East Africa, left in volcanic ash almost four million years ago.

(Below) The noble features of Waty have led to his being called "the oldest Egyptian mummy" (c.2400 B.C.). But the body inside his wrappings has decomposed and he is recognizable only because his plaster and resin-stiffened bandaging has set like a cast.

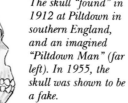

The skull "found" in 1912 at Piltdown in southern England, and an imagined "Piltdown Man" (far left). In 1955, the skull was shown to be a fake.

One of two jade burial suits made for a Chinese nobleman and his wife in the second century B.C. Their bodies decomposed, but the suits survived.

gilt-bronze headrest

MANY A PROSECUTION for murder has broken down because the corpse was missing, leaving only circumstantial evidence of a crime. Some of the world's most interesting bodies have disappeared in similar fashion, leaving only tantalizing traces of their passage through time. The evidence is particularly fascinating where it consists of "negatives" left in mud or plaster, like the earliest known hominid footprints or the impressions left by the victims of Vesuvius.

Sometimes there was no body there at all, as the history of fakes demonstrates. Egyptian embalmers, for example, having somehow lost a client's body, would bandage a dead baboon and pass it off as a child. As a subject for mythmaking, body and no-body are as powerful as ever in modern cult figures such as Count Dracula the Undead and H.G. Wells's Invisible Man, who must bandage himself, mummy style, when he wishes to make his presence known.

jade plaques linked by gold threads

Is this the garment in which the crucified Jesus was buried? Despite the image on the Shroud of Turin, in 1988 radiocarbon analysis showed that it was made in the Middle Ages.

dog tethered by collar and chain

monkey

A DOG from Pompeii, killed when Vesuvius erupted in A.D. 79. The victims' bodies decomposed, but casts could be taken by pouring plaster into the spaces in the solidified ash.

(Below) This wax effigy of Britain's King Charles II (1630–1685) stood on his coffin at his lying-in-state at Whitehall. Then, during the funeral procession, it lay in view on the coffin.

STORIES of mermaids (right) and mermen occur in many cultures. They are said to have been captured, and some even survive as "corpses" – made up of parts from many different creatures.

realistic modeled features

fish tail

ceremonial robes

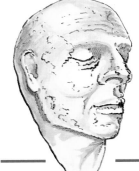

(Left) False teeth have often been genuine – taken from the dead or bought from the desperately poor. This set was owned by President George Washington (1732–1799).

(Left) Before the era of photography, the death mask – a plaster cast – was the most accurate way of recording a person's actual appearance. This is the poet John Keats (1795–1821).

Count Dracula, a "living" corpse who casts no mirror reflection.

A POSTHUMOUS BESTIARY

Frozen, embalmed, or stuffed, animals, too, have a history of mummification.

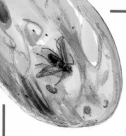

(Above) An insect which has been preserved in amber, a resin which has become fossilized.

CROCODILE mummies, bound and unbound. The ancient Egyptians mummified all kinds of creatures. Many were directly associated with their gods; the crocodile, for example, was identified with Sobek, the god of the water.

(Right) This baby mammoth perished some 44,000 years ago, but was preserved by the Siberian cold.

LIKE HUMAN BEINGS, creatures of many species have been preserved by accident or by design. The fossil record provides evidence of tiny creatures from the first phase of life on earth, as well as of those relative latecomers, the dinosaurs. But fossils are not bodies or mummies, since they mostly consist of minerals that have penetrated and replaced the bones and tissues. However, genuine remains of the prehistoric mammoth, an extinct relative of the elephant, have been found in the deep-freeze of Siberia.

The ancient Egyptians identified their gods with various animals, and respected the entire living creation; consequently they embalmed animals of all sorts, from scarab beetles to bulls. In South America, too, animals were mummified.

In more recent times animals have most often been stuffed, as trophies or museum specimens. Now, thanks to the new science of cryogenics, some pets will be preserved, just as they appeared in life, to console their bereaved owners.

(Right) A mummified baboon. In ancient Egypt, baboons, along with ibis, were sacred to the god Thoth. The Egyptians kept apes and monkeys as pets.

(Right) Preserved cat: the way in which the bandaging is woven in and out to form a geometric pattern is characteristic of around 50 B.C. The cat represented the goddess Bastet.

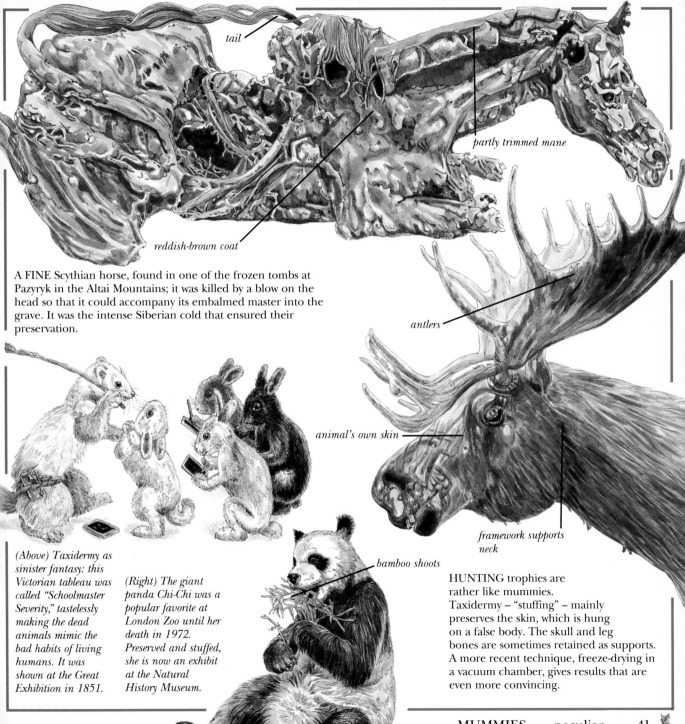

tail

partly trimmed mane

reddish-brown coat

A FINE Scythian horse, found in one of the frozen tombs at Pazyryk in the Altai Mountains; it was killed by a blow on the head so that it could accompany its embalmed master into the grave. It was the intense Siberian cold that ensured their preservation.

antlers

animal's own skin

framework supports neck

(Above) Taxidermy as sinister fantasy: this Victorian tableau was called "Schoolmaster Severity," tastelessly making the dead animals mimic the bad habits of living humans. It was shown at the Great Exhibition in 1851.

(Right) The giant panda Chi-Chi was a popular favorite at London Zoo until her death in 1972. Preserved and stuffed, she is now an exhibit at the Natural History Museum.

bamboo shoots

HUNTING trophies are rather like mummies. Taxidermy – "stuffing" – mainly preserves the skin, which is hung on a false body. The skull and leg bones are sometimes retained as supports. A more recent technique, freeze-drying in a vacuum chamber, gives results that are even more convincing.

THE MODERN STYLE

From the pyramid to the deep-freeze, the quest goes on.

(Left) The embalming of president Abraham Lincoln (1809–1865) gave the practice new prestige.

IN WESTERN SOCIETIES, embalming was for centuries an expensive and exceptional business, although kings and queens were often given the treatment. The last British monarch to be embalmed was Queen Victoria's predecessor, William IV, in 1837. Modern embalming methods originated in the eighteenth century, when the Scottish anatomists William and John Hunter devised the now standard procedure. It involves removing arterial blood and cavity fluids, and replacing them with formaldehyde-based solutions. However, embalming only became common during the American Civil War (1861-1865), when huge numbers of the dead needed to be preserved until they could be transported back to their families. The practice never became as popular in Europe.

Now those searching for immortality have another option. The science of cryogenics has given experts a new way of preserving bodies which involves subjecting them to temperatures only just above zero. This new deep-freezing procedure has led some people to believe that they can be kept on ice until science has developed new cures for diseases, and even for death itself.

draining body fluids

In 1924 the embalmed body of the Soviet leader Lenin (below) went on display in Moscow's Red Square.

Lenin's death mask

In the American Civil War, embalming enabled the dead to be taken home for burial.

Eva Perón (left) died in 1952. In 1955 her husband, the Argentine dictator Juan Perón, was overthrown. A political threat even in death, Eva and her silver coffin were "lost" for 16 years. Expertly embalmed, she was still striking in 1974, when she and Juan were reunited (right).

IN THE UNITED STATES, the departed is lovingly restored and often viewed.

A NEW BREED of pharaohs? People are already paying for places in vats of stainless steel, in which their bodies (sometimes just their heads) will be preserved in liquid nitrogen.

MUMMY FACTS

Why "mummy"? "Mummy" comes from the Persian word *mummiya*, meaning bitumen or pitch. Many badly embalmed Egyptian mummies were liberally doused with resins, which blackened over time, giving rise to the incorrect belief that bitumen was the embalming agent.

Sweet king Not all early embalming was done with salts and bandages. The body of Alexander the Great is said to have been on display for years in a glass coffin filled with honey. Sadly, we cannot be sure if this was true, although we do know that honey acts as a preservative.

Matter over mind Ancient Egyptian embalmers left the heart in the body, removed and preserved the other internal organs, but threw away the brains. Clearly they did not realize they were very important.

Tools of the trade Perhaps because bodies were not always sent for embalming very quickly, embalmers in ancient Egypt were not always certain of their clients' gender. In some instances they fitted body parts to a torso that forensic science has since shown did not need one!

Cat-astrophe In the nineteenth century a cemetery filled with embalmed cats was discovered at Beni Hasan in Egypt. They were shipped to Liverpool and processed to make fertilizers.

Fiery fate Irreverent later generations have used mummies for many purposes, including fuel for steam engines. American author Mark Twain (1835–1910) reported the fireman on one train as remarking "Damn these plebeians, they don't burn worth a cent! Pass out a king!"

Lucky dip A medieval Arab historian relates that treasure seekers feasted on a pot of honey which they found near the pyramids – until they got down to the perfectly preserved child floating in it.

VIP, RIP When the great warrior pharaoh Ramses II was flown to Paris for an operation he was 3,300 years old, had "monarch (deceased)" stamped on his passport, and needed treatment to halt the growth of fungus on

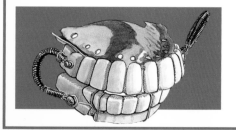

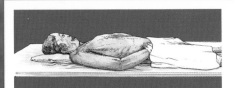

his spare, but still dignified, frame. The operation was a success.

Relative values Visiting the family meant something a little out of the ordinary in old Palermo, Sicily. Picnic parties regularly went to see their mummified relatives at the Capuchin convent, changing their clothes and discussing family matters with them just as if they were still part of the family.

Given the Gobi In 1978, sand-mummified bodies were discovered on the edge of the Gobi desert. The Chinese have kept very quiet about them, since the mummies seem to be European types – Bronze Age people, evidently in contact with China, despite the Chinese

tradition that their civilization was entirely homemade and free from all outside influences.

Explosive personality Lying in state at Whitehall, Queen Elizabeth I's body "burst with such a crack that it splitted the wood, lead and cere-cloth; whereupon next day she was fain to be new trimmed up." At least that was what one of the Queen's maids of honor said. However, her loyalty to the Queen was suspect, and she may not have been telling the truth.

A suitable case The jade burial suit on page 38 belonged to the Chinese noblewoman Dou Wan. Like her husband's suit, it consisted of over 2,000 jade plaques attached to one another by gold threads.

Posthumous pomp Inez de Castro secretly married Dom Pedro, heir to the Portuguese throne, but she was too humbly born for the reigning king's liking, and in 1355 he had her

murdered. Two years later Dom Pedro became king and ordered Inez's corpse to be enthroned with full honors.

Pick up or peck up? David Livingstone's African followers made an epic five-month journey to the coast with his body after his death in 1873. Then a warship came to pick it up and take it back to Britain. The ship was HMS *Vulture*.

God preserve his majesty! British monarchs and many royals were embalmed from the Middle Ages until the reign of Queen Victoria, who discontinued the practice.

The show goes on For six years after his death, the embalmed body of the great Italian tenor Enrico Caruso, who died in 1921, was on display in a glass coffin.

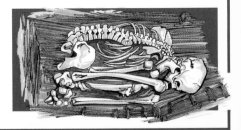

GLOSSARY

Adze Axlike tool with the blade set in the handle at a right angle.

Akh In Egyptian belief, one of the spirits released at a person's death; unlike others, it abandoned the body and flew to the stars.

Alchemy Chemistry in its pre-scientific phase, shot through with magic and imagination.

Amulet An object believed to offer magical protection to the person wearing it.

Anubis In ancient Egypt, the jackal-headed god of embalming.

Ba In Egyptian belief, one of the spirits released when a person died; it seems to have represented the character or personality.

Book of the Dead Western name for a collection of the spells and prayers placed in Egyptian tombs; for use in the dead person's journey through the underworld.

Bronze Age A prehistoric period between the Stone Age and the Iron Age, when bronze was used to make tools and weapons. It had reached Europe by 2200 B.C.

Canopic jars Set of four jars in which the ancient Egyptians stored the lungs, stomach, liver, and intestines of embalmed bodies.

Cartonnage Material of pulped linen, etc, resembling papier-mâché, often used to make the masks placed on Egyptian mummies.

CAT scanner Computerized Axial Tomography scanner: an advanced radiological machine that can give detailed information about mummies' insides.

Cryogenics The science concerned with temperatures near absolute zero.

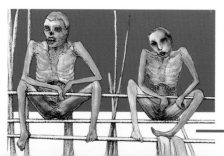

Egyptian history Starting from 3100 B.C., when Egypt was united under the first of 30 dynasties. Ancient Egyptian history is divided into several different periods. These are: the Old Kingdom (c.2686 to 1991 B.C.), the Middle Kingdom (1991 to 1567 B.C.), the New Kingdom (1567 to 668 B.C.), and the Late Period (668 to 332 B.C.).

Embalming The practice of preserving dead bodies.

Encaustic Painted with melted wax colors.

Endoscope Medical instrument for viewing the internal cavities of bodies.

Forensic Describes science or medicine used to explain legal or criminal matters.

Formaldehyde Preservative and antiseptic fluid, once very widely used.

Fossil The remains, or an impression left by them, of a plant or animal preserved in rocks.

Hominid A member of the human or human-ancestral family.

Incas The Indian peoples whose empire dominated the central Andes of South America from the thirteenth to fifteenth centuries. The center of the Incas's empire was Cuzco in Peru. The invading Spaniards, under their leader Pizarro, defeated the Incas in 1533.

Inuit Native North American peoples; Eskimos.

Iron Age Period that followed the Bronze Age. Characterized by the use of iron, the period dates from about 1500 B.C.

Ka In Egyptian belief, one of the spirits released when someone died, and homeless until the proper rites had been performed. It was a kind of double, resembling the dead person in every respect.

Kamiks Boots worn by Inuit.

Mummy A preserved dead body; originally applied to Egyptian, but now to any examples, including those preserved by accident.

Natron A kind of natural salt, found around the edges of lakes, used by the Egyptians for embalming.

Nazca culture A culture flourishing along the south coast of Peru, 200 B.C. – A.D. 500.

Opening of the Mouth Ancient Egyptian ceremony in which symbolic tools restored the dead person's senses, so that the spirit could return to the body.

Osiris Ancient Egyptian lord of the underworld and judge of the dead; supposedly the first mummy.

Papyrus A reedlike plant from which the Egyptians made "paper" and much else.

Posthumous After death.

Reliquary A container for holy relics.

Sarcophagus A stone coffin, usually very imposing and often intended to hold one or more wooden coffins.

Scythians A nomadic people who dominated the steppe lands north of the Black Sea from about the eighth to the third centuries B.C.

Sennet Popular ancient Egyptian board game.

Shabti In ancient Egypt, model mummy figures placed in tombs. They worked for the gods when required, in place of the dead person.

Subcutaneous Underneath the skin.

Taxidermy The preparing ("stuffing") and mounting of skins.

Torc Circular neck ornament of twisted, ropelike design. Sometimes spelt torque.

Trepanning A primitive operation in which a hole was made in the skull. A surprising number of patients survived the operation.

INDEX

Artists David Antram pages 8–9, 10–11, 12–13, 28–29, 32–33, 34–35, 42–43; Ray Burrows pages 22–23; Chris Etheridge pages 24–25; Gordon Munro pages 16–17; Lee Peters pages 38–39; Carolyn Scrace pages 14–15, 26–27, 30–31, 36–37, 40–41; Gerald Wood pages 18–19, 20–21.